JUST LET IT BE

With Acceptance Comes Healing

SHILPA GOEL

|| JAI MATA DI ||

To my daughter,
who has changed my life for good.

Dear God,
Thank You...
Thank You
for taking me through
troubled waters
and helping me
accept and cross them
by being present with me
in the form of
my family,
my friends,
my acquaintances,
my guides and mentors,
my idols,
the friends I lost,
and in the form of
the strangers whom
I met on my journey
but never stayed in touch with
and also,
sometimes in the form of
enemies who put me
back on my way
if I went astray.
Had it not been for
the troubles that I faced,

I wouldn't have learned
acceptance,
I wouldn't have grown
into who I am.
Thank You, O God,
Thank You.

1.

Our reality

We are not what
we appear on our Instagram stories
or on WhatsApp statuses.
We are the ones
lying on our bed,
the room engulfed in pitch darkness,
our face buried
deep inside our pillow,
sobbing uncontrollably,
muffling our voice
with our palm cupped on our mouth,
struggling for a breath
yet wishing not to take another breath.

We are not what
our perfectly filtered selfies
speak of us on social media.

We are those
anxious, self-loathing eyes
staring back from the mirror
at our imperfections,
when we wish to be perfect
not able to acknowledge that
those same flaws make us beautiful.

We are not those
laughing emojis
we send over chats.
We are those
lonely souls
talking to ourselves
on papers with ink
and crumbling them into balls,
tossing into the bin,
yet still afraid of pouring
all of ourselves
on those bits of papers.

We are not what
we show to the world.
We are what
we are afraid to show
even to ourselves.

2.

And one fine day,
the struggling fish
gave up on trying
to climb the tree.
She needed nothing more
to set herself free.

Let go of what's not meant for you

3.

You can be
a stone tower princess
or a wolf
running in the wild.
Make your choice,
let no one else decide.

You're amazing either way

4.

When God's reserved a diamond for you,
He'll make other stones reject you.

Rejections hold God's will

5.

Sounds of silence

Silence turns out to be magical
when you learn how to
listen to the voices
that your heart tries to put into words
but the noises of the world outside
keeps numbing the voices within.

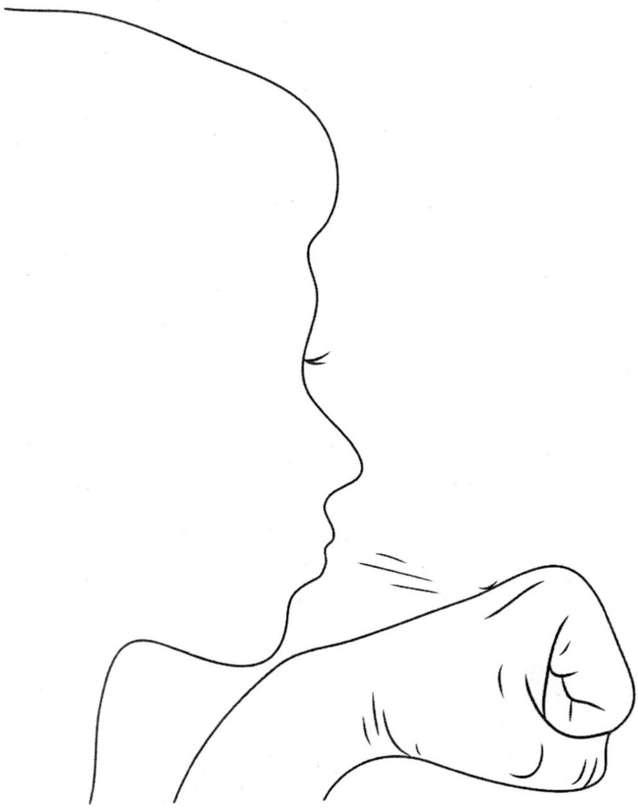

6.

Glory in falling

We were taught
to make wishes
on fallen things
be it
a falling star
or a fallen eyelash
yet we were never taught
that there can be
glory in falling
when it's meant
for giving someone
happiness, hope
and fulfilment.

7.

Hatred is admiration in disguise

You never know
how many people
admire you,
are inspired by you
just because
they are either
too shy to tell you
or they show it
in the form of hatred.

8.

Dark is important

If moon didn't go through
phases, how'd it become full?
If it didn't see the dark,
how'd it accept its scars?
You, my friend,
do not go through the dark,
you are taken through it
so that
when you see the light,
your vision doesn't get
blinded by the sight.

9.

Fears and fearlessness

Fears,
we all have them
whether we tell someone or not.
And hence, you're not alone.
That muscular guy
at your workplace
who fears no physical pain
might be too afraid
of feeling emotional pain.
That seemingly weak one
whom anyone can beat in
every physical competition,
might be so strong emotionally
and mentally having faced
the loss of his loved ones,
maybe his family.
The person who boasts

about fearing nothing and none
might be having his fears
buried in his heart
'cause our society has
tricked us into believing
having no fears makes us brave
and showing our fears
makes us a coward.
But the fearlessness is surely not
the absence of fears,
it is looking at your fears in the face
and telling them with all your heart,
"I'm stronger than you are."

10.

Pursuit of happiness

There's no definition
of happiness.
We can either
choose to be happy now
or we cannot.
But if we don't
choose happiness,
we would forever
keep chasing
the illusion of it.

11.

Flood of tears

When faced with an argument
with a loved one that turns into a fight,
you try to control your tears
but they betray you and flow like
a flood breaking through the dams
after being held back for a long time.

12.

Wear that
diadem of confidence
and be the queen
or the king
of your own world.

13.

Happiness doesn't always
come from within...
sometimes, happiness
simply comes from
seeing the other
person happy.

14.

"You've been given so much pain,
still, you don't hate me?"
asked the worried sharpener.

"You help me create art," replied the pencil.

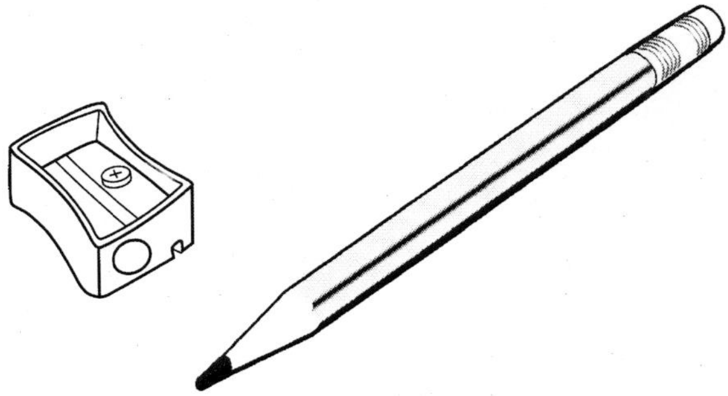

15.

Father

The root of the tree is often neglected
but how can a tree ever stay alive without the roots?
A father is that root of a family. He is almost always
taken for granted but there's no happiness in a
family whose roots aren't taken care of.

16.

Mom

There's nothing
she can't heal.
Body aching in sickness,
mind full of mess,
heart shattered into pieces,
but my head in her lap,
her hand on my forehead,
and every pain finds its way
back to where it came from.
Such is the power of
love and care of mom.

17.

A sad face doesn't affect me anymore
because I have seen smiles hiding sad faces
and that's heartbreaking.

18.

I am the kind of person
who will stand right next to you
when the world is against you.
Not because you are right
or wrong
or are my acquaintance,
but just because you are alone.

I know the pain of being left out.

19.

Yes, I am nice to you,
but don't expect me to
remain the same
when you start
taking me for granted.
My attitude doesn't
change like seasons
but it sure does change
as soon as yours does.
I am such a
"I will treat you
the way you treat me"
kinda person.

You get what you give.

20.

Famous life

Fame,
it doesn't come easy
and when it comes,
it brings everything with it
to make you feel like
you're doing something wrong,
to try to bring you down.

Fame,
it doesn't come easy
and when it comes,
it brings everything with it
to put you in depression.
You have people around,
You're lonely inside.
You will be gone
with no one by your side.

Your name will be left behind
but life?
Oh well, it went away
in worries and disguise;
disguises that you took
to be free from preying eyes.
You always wanted
to be known,
but now you wish
for an ordinary life.
You look at people
enjoying with families;
you, sit with tight security,
avoiding paparazzi.

Fame,
it doesn't come easy
and when it comes,
it brings everything with it
to remind you
how you ran behind

vain pursuits,
how fragile fame is,
how lifeless you became,
how public your life is.

Fame is good,
we all want it
but none of us wish
for the dark sides of it.

21.

And one day,
it will dawn upon you
how the circumstances
that seem to be against you
are actually the stepping stones
to the bigger favours
Universe has in store for you.

Stepping stones

22.

Ever observed
how losing something
you were afraid of losing
eventually sets you free?

23.

You found your Universe
in the wrong person because
you forgot that the universe
lies within you.

24.

Learn to accept your feelings.
If you won't be true to yourself,
how would you face the world?

25.

Don't let your grief
turn into anger.
Breathe.
Let your tears
pour on paper
and form words
of comfort.
I hope it makes you
feel better
and even if it doesn't,
at least, it will save you
the dire consequences
of unwanted anger.

Grief

26.

God will shut
the mouth of those
waiting for an opportunity
to humiliate you.

27.

When people start
leaving your life like
leaves falling off the trees
in the autumn.
Let them go because
spring surely comes along and
restore all those fallen leaves.

Stand tall

28.

When God loves you,
you don't need to
look for love
in the eyes of people.

Unconditional love

29.

The longer you cling to the memories,
the more you will suffer.

Free yourself

30.

Are you afraid
to hit the gym
because
people over there
would laugh at you?
But, my love,
isn't it the reason
you and all others
are present in the gym
in the first place,
to be in shape?
Why would they
laugh at you?
You chose to work
on improving yourself,
you should be looked upon
with respect.

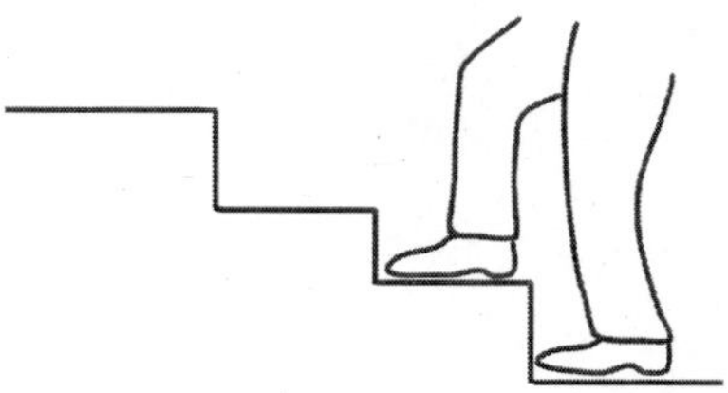

First step requires courage

31.

Maturity is when
the actions of other people
stop bothering you.
No matter what they do,
you just stop giving
a damn about it.

Maturity

32.

Art is universal;
it doesn't ask your age,
class, religion, race,
or any anything else.
It is inside everyone
who opens his/her heart
to the beauty of the world.

33.

Goals Meant for You

You set a goal
to grab a thing,
you try once,
you fail,
you try again,
you failed again.
Every time you try
the goal seems
even more unreachable.

But what if the goal
isn't really unreachable
but made so by God
only for you?
What if you think
that the very thing
you want to achieve

so you can be happy
might end up making
you miserable?
What if we give up
and leave things to God
for once?

He'll make it reachable
if it's meant for you.
You've tried hard already
to prove that you
deserve to own it
if it's meant for you.
And if not,
believe me that
God will definitely guide you
towards a goal
that is not only reachable
but you'd love
the journey of
attaining it too.

34.

Such a misfortune it is
to give up peace for possessions.
There's a peace in sacrifice
that greedy people can never find.

35.

Ignorance may give you peace,
But facing your fears brings
unbeatable strength.

36.

You cannot control
people and their emotions.
You cannot have
some people in your life,
if they do not wish
to stay in it.
And maybe that's what
life is about;
it goes on... and
we've got to leave behind
what we cannot control,
gathering our broken pieces,
moving ahead,
mending ourselves
on the way.

Keep going

37.

You deserve a pat on your back, too.
After all, it wasn't easy... you know,
holding on for so long.

38.

Adding filters to your selfies isn't important,

but adding them to your thoughts is.

39.

When I die,
I wish to be buried with
something that kept me alive.
I wish to be buried
with something to write.

40.

When they give you
a hundred reasons to cry,
show them that
you are blessed with
a million more reasons to smile.

Your smile kills them

41.

Weren't you heartless
when you intentionally
hurt a person
whose only intention was
to love you,
to make you their priority,
to make you feel special every damn time?
How can you have
such a person in your life
and still not feel lucky?
How?

Your loss

42.

Art:
the only balm
that can soothe
a broken heart.

43.

Let the words fill your heart
with each sunrise,
and let them pour on paper
as the night falls.

44.

You're not what you see,
you're not what you appear,
you're not what you hear,
you're not what you speak.

You ARE what you THINK,
and your greatest power is that
nobody knows what you think.

Your mind holds power

45.

If someone hurts you repeatedly,
don't fight with them.
Just walk away from their life
with dignity and grace.
My friend,
you deserve a better place.

Walk off

46.

When love is true,
there doesn't necessarily
have to be a relationship.
It can be from distance
and it can be really beautiful that way.

When fate separates

47.

Just spare a moment
to reflect on your imperfections
whenever you get an urge to
judge those of others.

48.

Sharing your emotions
with paper
is so much more comforting
than sharing with someone else.

People often judge

49.

You messed up,
you made a mistake,
it cannot be corrected
but not all mistakes
are meant to be corrected,
but every mistake you commit
is meant to teach you a lesson.
Running away from it,
not taking responsibility
for messing things up
can never teach you the lesson.
Accepting mistakes,
learning from them,
and not making the same mistake again
is what makes you human.

Take responsibility and learn

50.

The ones who break you do not possess
the divine power of making you.

Move on

51.

Beware! While waiting to hit the bull's eye,
you might miss out on all the darts
that could hit almost near it.
Dream big but do not miss out on
small opportunities.
Smaller milestones
reach to greater heights.

Stepping stones

52.

Untangling requires patience

Have you ever tried
solving a highly tangled wind chime?

Do you just pull out the strings
or be patient and sort out in sync?

When you mindlessly pull the knots,
they become an inseparable chaos.

While if you move the strings one by one,
seeing closely how they open,
with patience and perseverance, the wind chime
gets untangled after a while.

Life too is like a wind chime.
Problems become more intense
when we lose our patience.

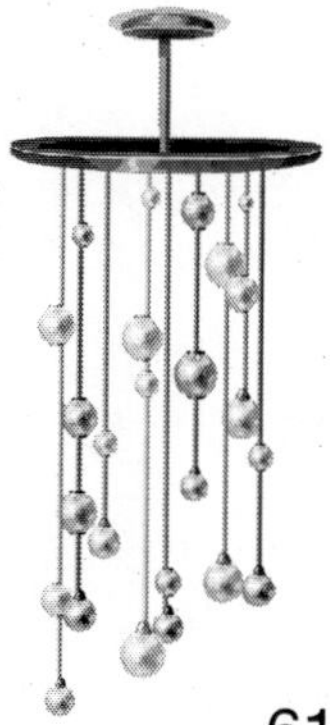

If we observe them step by step,
we can easily solve them
with a coordination between
heart, mind and time.

Also note that, the wind chimes get tangled
immediately after untangling with different knots
this time, and so do the problems in life.
Small or big, problems are always there in life,
always.

53.

The valleys of sorrow
disappeared
the day she fell
in love with
the person in her mirror.

54.

Let the child within you
unravel society's norms
from your mind,
let it live you the life
that's meant to be lived
according to your will.

55.

Have you ever felt so thankful to God or someone that you simply fail to know which word would be able to express your gratitude because *thank you* seems the smallest word ever? You open your mouth to say *thanks* but can't utter a single word because your heart is so full of happiness and overflowing with gratitude.

Believe me, it's the best feeling ever.

God's Grace

56.

When destiny gives you
the worst days of your life,
just have faith in God
and keep moving on and on.
Good times will come,
you've just got to be strong.

Sometimes faith is everything

57.

Let go of those
who hurt you
and make room
in your life
for those
who love you.
Fill your life
with beautiful souls
not beautiful faces.

Look within

58.

Temporary feelings cause
permanent damage.

Pause before you respond

59.

Be so busy

that you spare no time

hurting yourself

because of others' actions.

Your peace matters

60.

A skinny girl
and a curvy girl
stood facing each other,
cursing their own bodies,
wanting to look like
one another.
The skinny girl
wished for those curves,
and the curvy one
wanted to look like her.
Oh! How I wish
they fell in love with
the girls they saw
in their respective mirrors,
instead of cursing their own bodies
and wanting to look like others.

Embrace your mirror image

61.

To land on the moon
you have got to enjoy
your journey
through the stars.

One milestone at a time

62.

Every piece of a broken heart
becomes a weapon against love.

Turning cold

63.

It’s okay
if you dread
going to a workplace.
Find something
you can do from home
over phone calls,
emails and texts,
you’d still excel.

It’s okay
if you dread
going to the gym
or a park.
Get the yoga mat,
hit the YouTube
and burn those calories
at your home, in peace.

It’s okay

if you dread
going to the restaurant.
Just call your loved ones
and order something in,
or order in and eat
alone with your
favourite Netflix series.

It's okay
if you dread
going to the classes.
The internet is
full of study courses.
Just pick one,
pay for it
and learn from
wherever and
at whatever time
you want to study.

It's okay

to be not comfortable
in some places,
but it's not okay
to stop looking after
your health, desires, learning
and finances.

It's okay
to operate from home,
with the comfort of messages,
no verbal interactions,
no phone calls,
internet has it all.
Internet has given
my life a new meaning.

It's okay,
I do it all too
from my home.
Internet has been
the best invention

for the introverts like

you, me and so many more.

For us, introverts

64.

If angels turn out to be
the demons in disguise,
throw them out of your life
as soon as you can,
because
'it's better late than never.'

Backstabbers

65.

Let time

heal your wounds.

The scars will remain

a reminder of

the lessons learned.

66.

Isn't it strange,
how time flies
when you're happy
yet,
when you cry
your heart out every day,
days feel like years?

Is time an illusion?

67.

Don't know if
I am an emotional wreck
because I waste my emotions
on insensitive people
or
wasting emotions on
those people
made me so.

68.

Learn to love the pain
that comes from working hard
in pursuit of your dreams.
It signifies growth.

69.

“What would people say?”
These four words have
this wicked power of
keeping people from
achieving their dreams.

70.

How would you become
the number one
if you don't show
the courage to be odd.

71.

Clouds can only cover

the sun for some time,

they just can’t steal its shine.

72.

Believe in luck and destiny,
rely upon actions and plans.

73.

Healing takes time

The physical wounds
can be healed with
bandage, ointments
and medicines,
but when you heart is hurt;
when you feel pain
and it is visible to none;
when you feel numb,
falling each moment apart,
no one comes to heal you,
it's just you and your heart.
Now,
you can't wrap your heart
in a bandage or apply any ointment.
Your heart requires
a treatment of words;
your heart requires
the healing from time.
Time is the best healer,
doesn't matter how hurt you are,
eventually,
you come out of it.

You begin to live in the present,
you begin to accept reality.
You can't forget the past completely
but it gradually starts fading away…
fading away from your memories.

74.

Overconfidence

brings

fall.

75.

A step back
doesn't matter much
as long as
you're willing
to take two steps ahead
each time you lag.

Keep trying

76.

Pen and paper are your most reliable friends when you are an introvert in grief. The ink can embrace your pain like no one else. Because you know that if you start speaking, tears won't let you finish.

When voice breaks

77.

Parents

The only ones who stick around when everyone else leaves.

PS: Not if they are toxic and abusive. Yes, parents can be toxic, too.

78.

Your sad stories
turn into jokes
and tears into laughter
when shared with
your best friend.

That silly gem

79.

You change a lot over a year
by changing a little every day.

80.

How easy it is
to preach letting go.
Oh, how difficult
to follow it yourself.

81.

Strong are those
who aren't afraid of
being vulnerable.

82.

To be a writer
you just need
the audacity to
put your thoughts
and imagination on paper.

For aspiring writers

83.

I wasn't born an introvert

Maybe it was my fear
of being judged
that turned me
into an introvert.
They ask you to be
more expressive;
when you express yourself,
they pass their judgements;
when you try to justify your point
questioning their judgement,
you are suddenly
termed as outspoken.
So, you shut yourself up,
spending days in four walls,
cutting cords with people,
now happily calling yourself an introvert.

84.

People who don't know
the power of dreaming
will never value your dreams.

Stop explaining

85.

Forget the pain that people give you,
remember the blessings that
God showers upon you.

86.

It was all good
until
you fell in love with them
head over heels
and they...
they overlooked it.
It'll be good again
when
someone falls in love with you
and loves you the exact way
you deserve to be loved.

End the chase

87.

Your true friends will never come
between you and your progress.
They'd rather be the reason that
you grow far beyond your comfort zone.

88.

Writers feel every emotion
a little stronger and deeper than others
but we can't decide whether
it's a blessing or a curse.

89.

From crashing down
on bathroom floor at 3 AM
to putting yourself to sleep
at 10 PM every night,
you learned the art of self-love.

Art of self-love

90.

When your creator gave you the feelings,

He also gave you freedom to feel.

Don't suppress them

91.

And she often wonders,
if he hadn't been
a part of her life,
could her words
ever come alive?

Everyone is a blessing

92.

We are afraid of
the society and its constant
judgmental behaviour,
but…
aren't we a part of it?
Don't we contribute
to the society
and its judgements?
Pledge not to judge others
one person at a time
and the society
shall become
more accepting and
less judgmental itself.

Your mentality shapes society

93.

Get rid of
toxic people
else you'll drown
yourself in the
ocean of negativity.

94.

It doesn’t hurt you
to apologise when you’re wrong
and to say ‘thank you’
when someone’s been
nice to you.
Keeping that ego aside
and putting a stop on vain pride
can fill your life
with hearty smiles.

Keep it aside

95.

God is the best artist

What makes you think
you're not important?
What makes you underestimate
your existence?
God didn't give you
a unique face,
a unique identity,
a unique mind,
a unique body
just to see you
battling for your position
in this world.
He spent time creating you,
one of His artworks.
Respect yourself,
respect Him,
respect His art.

96.

They love you,
maybe they do not
but I don’t understand
why and how
does it stop you
from loving yourself?

Love yourself more when others don't

97.

Perfection doesn't mean
imposing your perception on others,
it comes when you keep
everyone's perspective in mind
while doing something.
Maybe that's why
it's just an illusion.

98.

Some people cross your life's path only to become a permanent resident of your memories.

99.

The inner critic lies to you
and the problem is
you listen and believe.

100.

You can't easily enter

the life of a person

who has mastered

the art of loving solitude.

Solitude is addictive

101.

Healing requires
a forgiving heart.

102.

Accepting difficult people
for who they are is tough,
even toughest, I know.
You're not alone.
But my experience says,
use silence as your weapon
as it kills them when
you don't react
to their non-sense.

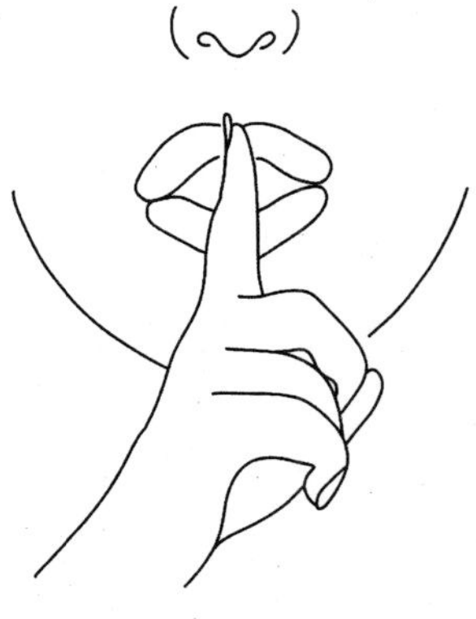

103.

And once in a while,
have the audacity to do
what others oppose.
You will instantly
come to know about
your haters hiding behind
the tag of ‘friends’.

True faces

104.

Having a heart satisfied
with the littlest you own
makes you a person
richer than the one
who owns the most
and still wants to hoard
more and more.

A content heart is a rich heart

105.

Some rare days are
too good to be true.
Those days when
you can't differentiate
between reality and dreams.

106.

A girl can endure any pain in the world but she can never tolerate tears in the eyes of her parents.

107.

Yes,
you're suffering.
Yes,
you're sharing it with someone,
talking provides you comfort
but
be careful,
the other person is suffering too.
Maybe they choose to not share it,
maybe they are not getting a chance at speaking,
or maybe they cannot speak about it at all.
Don't be so consumed by
your own life and talking about it
that you end up pulling others
into your own ocean of negativity.
Everyone suffers

108.

Taking care of yourself is self-love but caring about only yourself is selfishness.

109.

There's nothing better than
having a silent companion
on road trips,
amidst mountains
who enjoys their peace
and lets you enjoy yours.

110.

Brokenness will not only heal itself one day but also make your heart strong and wise enough to face any pain.

111.

Let them shine,
it's not your right
to dim anyone's light.

112.

How foolish of you
to think
they will keep loving you
even after
you repeatedly hurt them.
One day,
they will get tired of you
and move on
no matter how much
they loved you before.

Limits

113.

Moving on:

How difficult it seemed,

how relieving it turned out to be.

114.

If you can't appreciate
a new moon,
how would you value
the beauty of
new beginnings?

115.

There's difference of
only a letter between
anger and angel,
and yet
they can't exist together.

116.

We are living in a world where
loyal people can be counted on fingers.

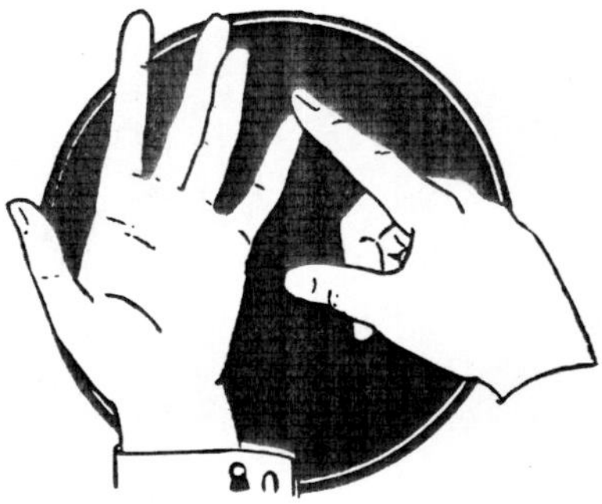

117.

There's someone out there
wanting to be as good as you are.

Stop complaining

118.

If emojis could reflect
our true emotions,
people would never be able
to send tears of joy
while crying in pain
behind the screen.

The veil

119.

The Greatest Artist

Go!

Yes! Now, go and

stand in front of the mirror.

Look at that creation

created by The Supreme Most Creator.

How can those flaws be not beautiful

when The Greatest Artist

gave them to you

to make you the most unique,

beautiful and one of a kind?

120.

Solitude helps you grow

Are you lonely?
Do you not have people around?
So what?
The day you learn
to love your company,
the power of solitude,
you'll never be lonely again.
You'll be alone, never lonely
and my friend,
magic occurs in silence,
in those moments of stillness,
in those moments of knowing yourself.

121.

All the love that you gave to a wrong person will return to you doubled and tripled from God. Just wait for your time.

Love magnified

122.

Some people leave your life to make space for the new and better ones. Don't stop those who don't want to stay.

Let them make space

123.

Inner peace comes when actions of other people stop bothering you. No matter what they do, you just stop giving a damn about it.

Choose peace

124.

It's not the memories you had with them that hurt... it's the unfulfilled desires that make your eyes well up with tears every time you think about your lost love.

Memories or desires?

125.

Arguments

Arguments,
I hate them
but also love them
at the same time.
When they're arguing with me,
trying to prove themselves right,
I take a chance
and keep learning things
by looking at the life
from their eyes
for they speak what they know
and what they see,
I keep placing my point
to keep the argument going,
to fire up their brain cells,
to make them spill
more and more knowledge

that I might not find

anywhere else.

I hate arguments,

I truly do

but they hide in them

gems of information too.

126.

Can someone be so selfish
that they turn
your love for them into hatred?
Yes, my friend, yes.

127.

Giving up is always
a better option than
holding on to something
that's not serving your soul.
If I hadn't given up on
a dream years back,
I wouldn't have found
the true calling of my soul.

It's okay to give up at times

128.

As long as you are willing
to achieve something,
nothing can stop you.
Your will power determines
how far will you go,
how satisfied will your soul be.

Power of determination

129.

The best things in life
come with expiry dates
and a hell lot of
terms & conditions.

130.

Broken cords

What do you do when
your cords with a loved one
are broken?
We all have broken cords
but the ones that hurt us the most
are the ones broken by
our beloved, our loved one
and we can do nothing
to fix the messed-up situation.
You accepted your mistake,
you have already apologised
but they are adamant
to break all the ties.

Just wish them the best,
you work is done.
If they do not wish to stay,
there's no use being stubborn.
Let them go,
find your peace,
the broken cords will

eventually be healed;
either they will return
or you'll find someone else...
someone who'll never break
their cords with you
ever... ever again.

131.

High volume

hurts ears,

but silence...

it deafens them.

132.

Nobody is worth the pain
that your heart feels.
So,
stop breaking your own heart
thinking all night
about the ones
who can’t see your worth.

133.

Losing you is
so much better than
that constant fear
of losing you.

To the ones who threatened to leave

134.

When the Universe decides to make your wish come true, no matter how bad the circumstances seem, your wish is definitely going to get granted because the Universe is working in your favour.

Universe is friendly

135.

Someone out there
wishes to have a
body like yours.
Someone out there
envies you for
who you are.
Someone tries to
pull you down
by making
offensive remarks
about your personality.
Know that, my friend,
people usually
try to degrade things
they desperately want to have
but can't work up
their level to get them.
You're enviably beautiful

136.

Life becomes
pretty easier when
you learn the difference
between hope and expectations.
Expectations hurt,
hope doesn't.
Hope for everything,
expect nothing.

Expectations hurt

137.

Do you just
look at someone
and wonder
what amazing things
did you do
to deserve them in your life?

That one person

138.

Sometimes you live more in the memories than you live in the present. Is that why you're sensitive towards goodbyes or does it happen because you ARE sensitive towards goodbyes? So sensitive that tears come rolling down your cheek on their own, no matter how much you try to control them.

Goodbyes hurt

139.

How easy it is to make fun of someone,
how difficult to step inside their shoes.

140.

You're one of a kind,

never let your uniqueness die.

141.

Who do you cry for?

You,
I hear your voice in the morning,
it sounds sore.
Your eyes seem swollen,
your vision must be blurred
for I see you rubbing your eyes
every now and then.
You cried last night,
didn't you?
No, don't lie.
I know you cried,
you cried your heart out.
To whom?
To the One sitting above,
claiming to be looking over
all of us?
To the One who we look for

in every trouble, in every grief
hoping He'd listen to our prayers?
If yes, then stop crying.
And by the way,
Who do you cry for?
For the one who had promised
to be by your side
in every phase of your life?
Or for the one who
showed you the dreams of forever
and left in the blink of an eye?
Or
for the one who seriously
doesn't give a damn about you;
the one who said you meant the world to them,
and now, your tears are your only companion
when you need them the most?
Look, listen,
stop crying to the One sitting above,
stop crying for the one who didn't deserve your
love,

stop crying and give yourself some time.
Take that night and embrace solitude.
Sleep is comforting,
don't waste a night crying.
Don't pity yourself,
pity the one who never valued your love.
Cheer up and know that
your heartbreak brought you a step closer
to the one who truly deserves you.

142.

You might meet
people in life
whom you'll get
attached to.
The ones who'll
destroy you and leave;
who won't even
bother to ask someday...
if... you are... okay.

People we meet

143.

A story doesn't end
until it has left you
at peace with yourself.
If a story left you
craving for more,
then don't worry
and hold on,
there's usually
a sequel to that one.

Wait and watch

144.

If your little heart
is strong enough
to pump your blood
perfectly even when
it's broken,
why can't you
carry on with your life?

Be strong

145.

You know,
the tragic stories
are usually the ones
that become immortal.
Romeo and Juliet,
for example.
After all,
it's a broken heart
whose ink bleeds
the deepest emotions.

Penning pain

146.

Sometimes
you may have
all the happiness
and still feel sad.

147.

Whether they love
a man or a woman,
whether they are
lesbian, gay, trans or bi,
loving someone
is entirely their choice.
Let's just learn to respect
the love of all kinds,
and put an end to raising
questions on others lives.

Love is love

148.

A fruit was plucked from some branch of some tree... but it left the whole tree in pain.

A daughter's wedding

149.

Why try to fit into a glass shoe to be a princess
when you can be a misfit and still be the queen.

150.

The art of being calm

Being calm is an art
I do not possess.
I lose temper at
all the little things,
maybe you do too.
I try, I try a lot to not react
but to just look at and observe
the circumstances, yet
I eventually lose control,
maybe you do too.
I can only say that
you're not alone,
I am not alone.
There are people in the world
who are like me,
who are like you,
who are like us,

but we can't stay stuck here.
Let's learn that art
together, one step at a time,
let's pledge to not give up,
to keep trying.

151.

People usually crave for food and parties,

And I?

I crave for road trips and mountains.

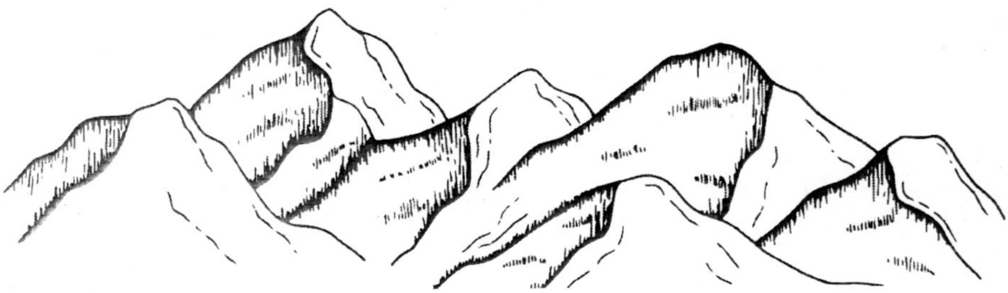

152.

Pretending to be perfect by hiding your flaws just insults the human being whom God has created.

153.

If you feel like God isn't listening to you just because what you want the most isn't coming to you, look at the other prayers that He answered. Maybe what you are asking for is too dangerous for you. God always knows better.

Trust him

154.

Love can't be toxic

If someone’s constantly toxic towards you,
feel no shame in walking away from them.
Your peace is far more important
than your love for them.

If you’re toxic towards someone,
recognise, accept, apologise.
Either change your attitude
or walk out of their life.

‘cause, my friend,
love is free of toxins.
If either of you is toxic,
it’s not love, it’s just a relationship.

155.

There's nothing beautiful about a heartbreak, but there's so much beauty in how you hold on to your pieces and glue them back together to form a stronger, wiser heart.

156.

If you'll do good to me,
I'll return with the best.
But if you do bad,
your karma will do the rest.

Not messing with your karma

157.

Ignite those
flames of faith
once again in your heart.
Fears need some rest too,
now put them aside,
at least, for a while.

Let fears rest

158.

Redefining Beauty

Those stretch marks,
yes,
the ones you hide.
Why though?
Why do you hide them?
Wear them with grace
for they signify your
divine transition to motherhood,
often your hustle at the gym.
Wear them with grace
for they show
how amazingly you've grown.

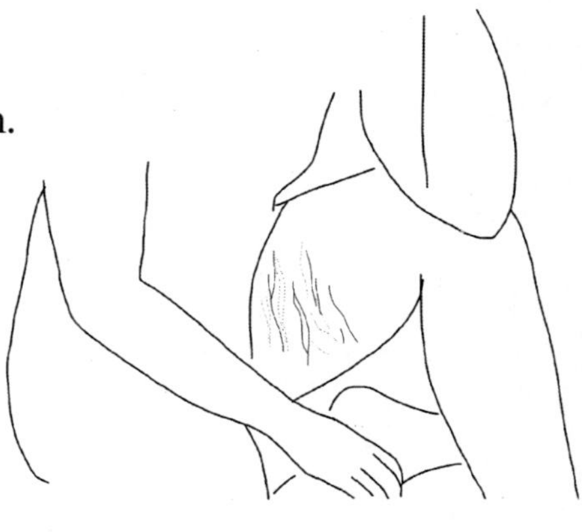

159.

Not everyone will understand
when you tell them that
you're anxious or depressed
but someone will surely do,
hold them close to you.

It's okay to open up

160.

That pressure,
That stress,
That pain,
none of it is bad
as long as
you're willing
to grow under it,
as long as
you desire
to shine
like a star.

Willpower

161.

So many people
tried to turn you selfish
for they snatched so much from you
just by being selfish,
and you...
you still couldn't learn selfishness
no matter how many things
you had to let go of.
'cause, my friend,
pure hearts
cannot be damaged
by the greed of others.

Selfishness

162.

The one light that always guides you to your right path is the one that appears before you during your darkest times. And that's the only light which is visible to you at that time.

The guiding light

163.

A creator doesn't cause destruction... until their patience is tested, until you force them to do so, until the destroyer hidden inside them is provoked... and then, they sure do destroy in a way that you can't even think about.

Creator turned destroyer

164.

Sometimes, you witness a moment that is too beautiful to be described in words. So divine that you just want it to remain in your heart because when you try to tell someone about it, its essence gets lost somewhere.
The listener would never understand the depth of that moment because they never saw it, never felt it.

Moments that can only be felt

165.

Don't let ego ruin your relationship. Just because love came easily to you, don't take it for granted. You never know the number of lovers striving for the love of their life. Love never came easy to them, and they know how to value it once blessed with it.

Valuing love

166.

Destroying someone's life and
then not even thinking about them,
must be some kind of sin,
easy to carry out,
but too difficult to repent.

Sin

167.

Daddy's little princesses
may find their prince
earlier than you,
but a queen has the patience
to build her kingdom
and let her king arrive
in his own time.

Be the queen

168.

Some bonds are too strong
to be broken by
misunderstandings,
people,
separation,
circumstances,
or even timings.
There's some Godly force
keeping them together
beyond every trouble.

Divine relationships

169.

Sometimes,
you just have to
let them go
if you want them
back in your life.
Universe grants wishes
in strange but
most beautiful ways.

Law of attraction

170.

There's a different story
written for everyone.
Stop living
someone else's life
else,
you'd just be
the plagiarised version
of them.

Plagiarism

171.

Innocence

The thing about people
with an innocent heart
is that
they trust anyone
who shows little affection,
little care towards them;
they open up to others
and share their secrets,
thinking the other person
carries a heart
as beautiful and pure as theirs.
Unfortunately,
they either
end up being judged
or
their innocence is
used against them.

172.

God knows
perfect timing
for everything
and everyone.
So, relax
and
sit back
to enjoy
His miracles.

Miracles of God

173.

Sometimes,
the end is
not actually the end.
It's just God's way
of saying,
"hold on,
you haven't lost them.
They are taking
a detour to your life.
This seeming end,
O tired soul,
is just a resting point
for your perseverance."

Hold on

174.

As we grow up,
we stop being afraid
of ghosts and spirits,
because we finally learn
that even if ghosts exist
they aren't scary
or mean any harm to us,
dangerous are the humans
who possess a dark mind
and pretend to be nice.

The real terror

175.

When you see someone
with multiple feathers on their cap,
don't sit there counting the feathers
and envying the person.
Instead, look at them
with awe and be inspired,
trying hard to earn
even more for yourself
because, my friend,
if they can,
you can too.
No dream is big enough
if you're determined to
achieve it with all your heart.

176.

Each wave tells a story

Witnessing
someone's woebegone days and
someone's blissful smile,
each wave that
comes to the shore
returns with a story to tell.

Couples holding hands,
walking along the shore.
A wave comes to wash their feet
and takes back with her
their sorrows, their worries.
Each wave that
comes to the shore
returns with a story to tell.
A kid playing with the ball,
warned by parents

to not go near the shore.
A wave comes and
kisses her little feet;
her giggle feels fresher
than the morning breeze.
Each wave that
comes to the shore
returns with a story to tell.

Watching fishermen
preparing their boats,
the wave that
comes to the shore
returns with a heavy heart,
anticipating her fishes' fate.

Each wave that
comes to the shore
takes back with her
a pocket full of stories

to share with her

marine friends.

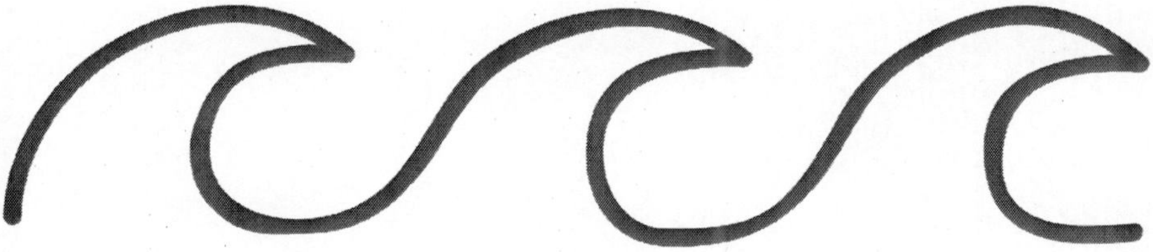

177.

You rise in life by helping others rise,
no one ever became great by pulling someone else down.

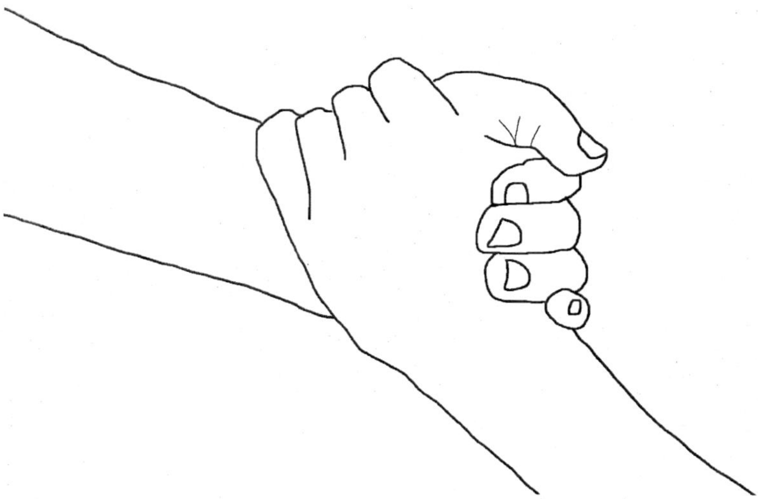

178.

Rude and blunt people usually hide their golden hearts,
fear those who behave too good on your face.

179.

Their hatred,
their opinions,
their bullying,
their contempt,
it was all intended
to sabotage us.
But there was
something worse.
We let them succeed
‘cause we let their words
become our thoughts
about ourselves
and it all became
self-destructive.

If only
we had ignored it all
and believed in ourselves more,
their attempts would be vain

and there wouldn't be any
self-elevated pain.

Self-sabotage

180.

Those who believe in Santa
do not have to wait for Christmas
to have their wishes fulfilled.
The true power lies in believing.

181.

Your eyes are
so beautiful,
so intense.
Tell me
what tragedies
enchanted them,
how many tears
have they shed?

Tragedies

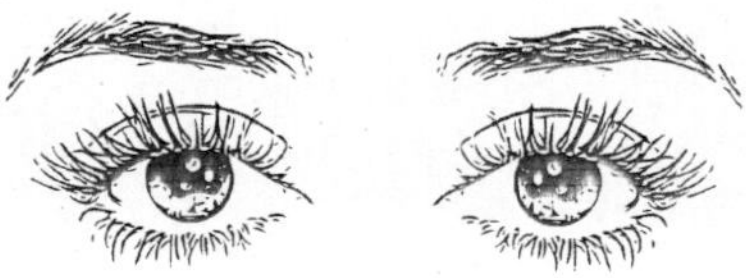

182.

Life's meant to be
lived in the present,
not to be wasted
in awaiting future.

Note to self

183.

Don't let
the winter in your head
stop the spring
that's trying
to arrive
in your heart.

184.

There comes a time
when you get tired
of asking people to stay;
when letting go becomes
easier than holding on;
when you finally learn
that you deserve more.

185.

I could sing
the melancholies
of my sorrows
but instead,
I choose to
celebrate
for every ending
marks a
new beginning
and
I SHOULD WECOME IT.

186.

You know that
they weren't
nurturing your soul
when you feel
thankful for their
forgotten memories.

187.

Getting burned down
isn't the curse.
The inability to
rise from the ashes is.

Phoenix

188.

Don't love so much that

your love becomes

suffocating for your beloved.

Over possessiveness

189.

How I love being with
imperfect people;
original, flawed
just like me.

190.

In order to truly liberate yourself,
you have got to rid your heart of
hatred and fears.

191.

We all are nothing but
the puppets of our mind.

192.

I wish some memories could fade
faster than they were made.

193.

You know when you have something
you are absolutely in love with,
almost like an obsession,
the right ones help you make it your strength
while the wrong ones use it as your weakness.

194.

"Why are you so kind to everyone you meet?" they asked.

"It's simple. I have nothing better to offer them than kindness," I replied.

195.

A heart in pain is much stronger than
an unscathed heart, unaware
of any kind of pain.
The latter carries only the philosophies
about treating others the right way,
the former carries experience.

196.

Out of misery

often come blessings.

197.

Letting go of someone
you love with all your heart
comes with such strength
that it liberates you from
temptation and attachment
of all kinds in this world.

198.

When you love someone,
their name itself
becomes an emotion.

199.

There are two ways:

1. Make other children go through the issues that you faced in your childhood, so that you take your revenge. The negative and the wrong step.

2. Spread awareness and make world a better place so that no child goes through what you went through. The positive and the right step.

And between right or wrong, choice is always yours.

200.

You're beautiful, you know?
Maybe people's eyes are not
beautiful enough to behold.

201.

To look your best

wear your courage and confidence.

202.

An introvert's journal speaks
much more words than
an extrovert's mouth ever will.

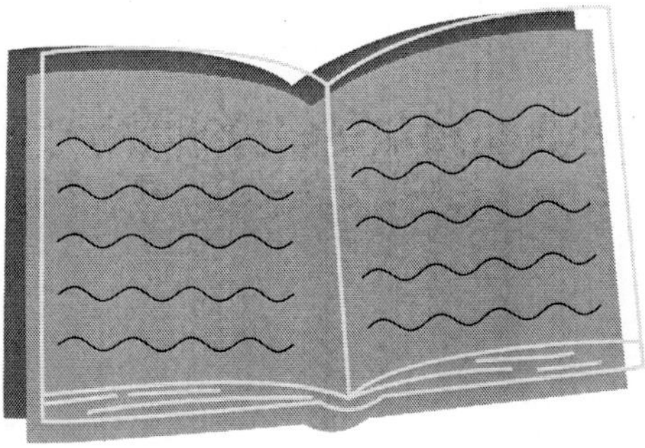

203.

Do you see
that chasm present
somewhere between
fiction and reality,
yes...
that's where
the bookworms reside.

204.

Enchanted

Talk to me about
the beauty of the moon
and the shine of stars,
about
the greatness of the mountains
and the vastness of oceans
talk to me about
the impeccability of the landscapes.
Fairy tales don't enchant me
'cause I am habitual of finding
magic in nature.

205.

How to write a poem

Let loose your emotions,
pour them on paper,
feel every fibre of it
till nothing is left unsaid.
Go back in time,
make those memories come alive.
Take the canvas of your diary
and let your ink bleed fearlessly.
Make nature your friend
and hatred your foe
'cause it's a heart filled with love
from where the words flawlessly flow.

206.

Pain today, strength tomorrow

‘Pain’
a four-letter word,
but isn’t ‘grow’
a four-letter word too?
Pain seems to break you
but it actually makes you.
Pain it is today, yes,
but the same will be
your strength tomorrow.

Cry...
cry as much as you want to
but then, stop and know that
the pain’s got a purpose to serve too.
Face it, accept it and then,
grow through it.

This brokenness today
will be receiving
all your gratitude tomorrow.

207.

When you know you're right,
be unapologetically right.
When you know you're wrong,
Be brave to accept it.

208.

Just because you don't know about
the sufferings of the others
doesn't mean that
every person isn't suffering
in one form or the other.
You're not alone to suffer.
It's okay to share with others
and it's important to be kind.

209.

Don't judge their beauty,
judge your vision instead.

210.

My tears make me strong,
don't mistake them for my weakness.

211.

They kill your confidence

and ask,

“why aren’t you confident enough?”

212.

Dreams get broken;
everyone's dreams
get broken at least once.
But sometimes,
our dreams break
because we let
people's judgement
weigh more in importance
than the need to
achieve our dreams.

We let people break our dreams

213.

Having loved and lost too many people,
what can I be if not kind?

214.

It is a blessing to have someone
who plays multiple roles in your life.

215.

Don't get attached to people who are
habitual of giving up on the things they love.

216.

Words can be your
best friend or worst enemy.
Choose them wisely.

217.

We're are expected
to live a life…
a secure life
with a high paying job,
a family of four
and to not to listen to our soul.
I never chose
a creative life
but I'm grateful
that it chose me.
This, somehow, feels
a more secure place
than a life with
family, friends and job
because…
it truly soothes my soul.
On creative life

218.

People who stay awake the whole night
sitting under the stars
have so many deep conversations
buried in their heart.

219.

Maybe God too has to be
stubborn at times
to not answer our prayers
and show us
the right path instead.

220.

In today's world,
being kind-hearted feels
more like a curse.

Still, choose kindness

221.

Some voices scare you at goodbyes
because you will never hear them again.
Some other voices scare you during goodbyes
because when you hear them again someday,
they will bring back the times that
you are trying so hard to get over with.

222.

Sometimes alone
is not the best
place to be;
the memories that you
keep running away from
come trickling down
your face from your eyes.

223.

Every unfulfilled wish
made me furious,
yet the same wish
made me grateful
when I learned
why it was not fulfilled.

224.

The moon shone in its full glory

no matter how many wolves howled at it.

225.

If the rain cared about the haters,
it would have disappointed Pluviophiles.

226.

I finally started finding ways
when I realised the ill-effects
of making excuses.

227.

The brain kept winning battles,
but somehow,
the heart won the war.

228.

I am afraid of the dark souls,
not dark places.

229.

"What hurts the most?" they ask.
"When you have no choice but
going back to being strangers again," came the reply.

230.

The eyes that matter

Did you lose
someone you loved
to someone else?
I understand,
it might have hurt
a damn lot
but listen, dear soul,
be proud.
Be proud because
God chose you
for making the sacrifice.
He knew you're strong enough
to go through his tests.
Be proud because
in His eyes,
you're not
a selfish soul.

231.

The so-called spot
on the moon
just enhances its beauty.
Oh, how boring
it would have been
had it been spotless.

You don't have to be flawless

232.

It's when you start attracting only the best people do you realise that the ones who left also took their negativity along.

233.

Flaws

When you point out
someone's flaws
and try to mock them,
they remain the same,
nothing would make
them lesser than you
but...
it sure will add
a flaw to yours;
the flaws of not knowing that
their flaws make them beautiful
but making fun of them
sure does make you awful.

234.

If someone puts you down
for feeling good about yourself,
don't spend a minute more
on them or their nonsense.
No use talking back,
no use stooping to their level,
just walk away from them
like they never existed,
like they never mattered.

Value yourself

235.

When you're tired
give yourself a break.
Else you'll keep
pushing beyond limits
and break yourself.

Breaks prevent breaking

236.

Just because
the world didn't see your worth
doesn't mean that
God didn't see it either
'cause it is not by chance
that you took
birth in this world.

You are worthy

237.

Judgements

When you cry,
people call you weak.
When you fight back,
they call you a rebel.
When you try to put your point,
they brush it aside
mocking you by saying,
"you're pretending to be wise."
When you stay silent,
they keep provoking you
until you speak up and give them
a reason to say something.
People will always have
a problem with you,
your behaviour,
your actions,
your words, values, beliefs;

people will always find

a way to attack

your sincerity.

Don't let them change

any of these.

Just react the way

you feel is

a wise way to react.

238.

Every time you
poke your nose
in other's business,
you lose a chance
at minding your own.

Priorities

239.

Our gratitude towards God (or Universe) goes two ways:-

- One, when we start being grateful when we start getting more than we asked for.
- Two, we start receiving much more than we asked for when we remain grateful for what we already have.

I choose to live by the latter, what about you?

Ways of being thankful

240.

Loving and losing

We loved,
we lost.
Our hearts
turned cold.
We loved again,
we lost again.
Our hearts turned colder
and we turned our faces
away from God.
And then,
a series of events
revealed how significant
were the lessons that
we learned during
our phases of
loving and losing.
We loved yet again,

unfortunately,

we lost them this time too.

But also, this time,

our hearts turned kinder,

we ran under God's light,

we learned to appreciate life,

we learned to appreciate

the love of all kinds.

241.

Our only limitation is that
we only believe
what is visible to our eyes
and audible to our ears.

There's more to this world

242.

The bitter truth is,
most of the people in our life
are temporary, nobody stays.
The good thing is,
they are almost always
replaced with someone far better.

Replacement

243.

Out of all my flaws,
the worst is giving
all the importance
to the people
who least deserve it.

Messed up priorities

244.

You went through
hell and back,
nobody accompanied you there,
did they?
So, why do you
allow them to
belittle you
or your achievements?
You know yourself
and your life,
to make you feel
little of yourself
nobody's got the right!

They don't have the right

245.

Ask a lone billionaire if it hurts or not to have all the money but no family to share it with.

246.

Diaries don't remain just diaries once inked with emotions. The words become their soul.

247.

Knowledge can be gained by anyone from anywhere but using your knowledge wisely is the real game.

248.

Dreams require actions and planning too.
Just sitting and dreaming lead you nowhere.

249.

The stories behind the scars

Are you ashamed
of wearing those scars?
May I ask you why?
Is it because
they have a story to tell
of your loss,
of your pain,
of your struggles,
bravery and life?
You didn't get those overnight,
that huge scar which you hide
once costed you almost your life.
You didn't invite those scars,
they came before
you could even see them coming,
and became your permanent part.
Wear them proudly, my friend,

for they tell stories of your

life, loss and struggles.

250.

Cheating does as much damage to a man as it does to a woman. Just because men appear stronger doesn't mean they are not broken from inside.

251.

And who says that honesty is alive,
I have seen the drunks speaking lies.

252.

They will show you dreams,

Then they will break ~~your dreams~~ you.

253.

The biggest lessons you learn in life is when you lose your loved one. Give time to pain, it may fade but keep those crucial lessons with you till the end. If time is the best healer, then loss is the greatest teacher.

Learn and heal

254.

You know which is the worst kind of pain?

It's when you heart cries,

But tears fail to reach your eyes.

255.

Picking up the pieces

They were scattered all over
you know, the pieces of
my broken glass heart.

I let them hurt my soul
every now and then
whenever I stepped over them.

Then I decided to
clean up the mess,
gather my pieces,
to glue them back.

It hurt, it hurt a lot.
Each piece pierced as
memories came flashing back.

Once it was done, I realised
the new and wiser heart
was worth the agony
I underwent all this time.

256.

One day
you'll get tired
of giving all your love
to the wrong person
and that will be
one of the best
days of your life.

Freedom

257.

If God takes away
one of your reasons
for happiness,
He's giving
a million more
in return...
look for them,
they are present
everywhere.

258.

First impression isn't the last

Is first impression truly the last?
In one meeting, we can't judge someone's attitude and class.
If in the first meet, two people maintain silence,
their judgement is then merely based on appearance.
To know a person well,
you've got a make a move and dwell on their views,
talk face to face and share your views too.
Then only you can know their value.
Someone might appear rude at first,
but you never know they may be having the softest heart;
while some other might seem a gem at first meet,
though they are filled with all the evil.
Still, for a majority of people, alas,
the first impression is truly the last.

259.

Be grateful for the things
that others envy you for
rather than envying others
for the things you don't have.

260.

Even if people
are blind to your efforts,
God isn't.

261.

Carry courage and confidence

It's your body,
you know well
what suits it
and what not.
If you're comfortable
in a dress,
let not anyone tell you
if it's good or bad.
If you feel confident
in a particular dress
but people are
quick to tell that
it's inappropriate
or that you don't carry it well,
just turn your ears deaf
and ignore their comments
because, my friend,

you look the most beautiful
when you carry courage,
comfort, confidence,
and a healthy pride in your eyes
accessorised with a smile
that can light up anyone's life.

262.

The perfection on social media
can deceive you beyond measure.
You have no idea
of the story behind their apparent treasure.
We all pretend to be perfect
on those temporary 24-hour stories and posts
hiding behind them the acts that
we carry out to click pictures and record videos.

Social media is deceptive

263.

Beauty fades away,

intelligence lasts forever.

Brain over beauty, always

264.

"Time heals everything" is
as true as clichéd it sounds.

265.

Dear best friend,

Whenever I mention the word ‘family’, know that you’re already counted.

266.

It's the memories that keep a person alive in someone's heart.

267.

Some nights were dark,
the moon didn't appear.
Some days were dull,
the clouds hid the sun.
But they never doubted
the capability of
the sun and the moon
to shine in their time.

Shine when it's your time

268.

Focus on your personality,
it speaks louder than
your height, weight
or the colour of your face.

Be you

269.

As long as
your reflection in the mirror
smiles back at you,
you are perfect.

Let you be your first love

270.

Since I went through that phase,
I know I can face any pain
and be aware that
it too will fade.

271.

Chase the dreams
that your heart
wants to achieve
not the ones that
others make you see.

272.

Your heart is allowed
to break over and over again
but make sure that
you mend it each time,
not let it turn cold in pain,
and the reason for which it breaks
is never ever the same.

Let pain teach you

273.

The doors that aren't meant for you
won't open, no matter for how long
you keep banging on them.

It's okay to give up at times

274.

Silence of early morning,
echoes of lonely mind,
I got to know what's true bliss
when I embraced my alone-time.

Solitude is bliss

275.

Early mornings hide
magical moments in them.
For once,
kick off that blanket,
jump out of the bed
and
absorb the beauty of the sunrise.

Magical moments

276.

Society killed that child

You're holding too tight
onto the ideas that
society dumped in your mind,
aren't you?

Be a kid again,
unlearn everything that
stops you from being you.
Unlearn the things that
stop you from chasing your dreams.
The kid in us knew
we were meant to be great,
but the society pushed
a lollipop of rules and limitations
down our throat
and choked that
unconquerable child in us

to death.
And hence,
we grew up learning
that we can never be
the hero of our life.
Alas!
What a tragedy
being a part of
this society is.

277.

Light up the heart of a person
whose smile doesn't reach his eyes.

278.

Keep shining even if
your light pierces
the eyes of some people.
And then, shine even more.

279.

When you buy things
that you need to utilise
in order to become
a better version
of yourself,
it's an investment.

Invest in self-development

280.

Happy souls are
the ones who
identify and accept
their imperfections.

281.

Stop picking up love from people

like coins thrown before a beggar.

282.

In today's world,

you can be either kind or honest.

283.

Be the odd one

You wish to rise
above others
but...
you're not willing
to accept that
people who can't
rise themselves
would do their best
to stop you from rising.
You'll have to ignore them
when they call you crazy
for spending time indoors,
working on your dream
rather than partying.
You'll have to be proud of yourself
when they call you insane
for believing in all the things

they are cynical about.

You will be odd

in their eyes

but know that

you cannot be number one

if you cannot show

the courage to be odd.

284.

Moon has to go through the phases,
it can’t stay full each day
no matter how much he wants to.
You, my friend, too
do not have to be
at your best each day.

Every day is different

285.

Attachments with some people
can never be broken.
Our soul is connected with theirs.

286.

You know
you went astray
when you became
indifferent towards
permanent things
while chasing
the temporary ones.

The wrong path

287.

Often happiness is
just a cup of tea away.

Small joys

288.

They making you feel good
and they being in love with you
are two different things.
Don't fall for someone
just because
they make you feel
like nobody else.

Love is more than just feelings

289.

You can't let yourself drown

in the pool of their lies.

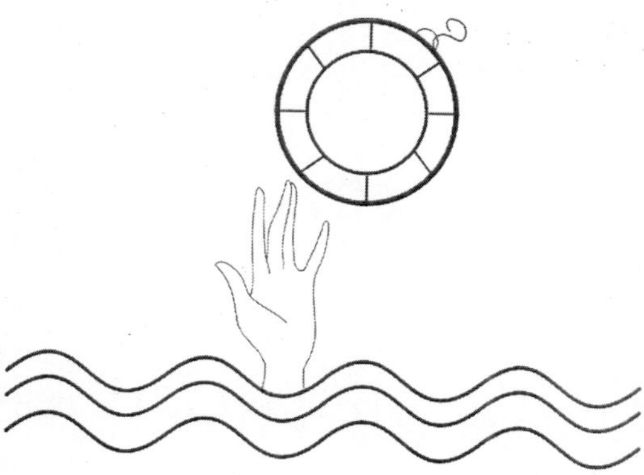

290.

There's a strange peace
in behaving nice with people
who have a troubled soul.

291.

Be there for yourself

You'll be called names;
you'll be called ugly,
fat or just skinny.
People will try their best
to fill you with doubts
about yourself,
and that's when
you'll need yourself the most.

Look into the mirror
and fall in love with the person
over and over
till you just can't stop loving
the person that reflects back
at you from the mirror.

Whenever you're dragged down,
know that people have a habit of
dragging beautiful souls down.
It's in your hands
to let them use

it as your weakness
or your can trash
their vain opinions
and take yourself
on a beautiful journey
of self-love and self-care.

292.

When you lose someone to whom you were too attached emotionally... nobody will ever know how you feel when each memory of them keeps visiting your heart every now and then.

Indescribable feeling

293.

We cherish memories
more than relishing
the present moments.

294.

Silence bears more wrath than a barking mouth.

295.

Yes, I'm an Introvert

Yes, I am an introvert
and I am not ashamed of it.
I do stay in most of the times
and I do love it.
I do not interact with many people
but to whom I do,
I am with them completely
honest and true.
When my energy starts draining
I do leave conversations in the middle
but there are those too
whom I never get tired of talking to.
I am rude at times
sometimes, I am blunt too,
I never mean to hurt anyone
but sometimes, I unintentionally do.
I do not dislike going out,

I too love to step out of my home,
but I require my chosen company
because I hate going out with people
who are not inside my comfort zone.
Yes, I am an introvert
and I hate a lot of people
but those whom I love,
I love them with all my heart.
Trickery, treachery and betrayal
are not my cup of tea,
I prefer being alone than
having some fake company.
There's nothing wrong with me,
nothing at all,
I just choose not to adjust
in a world full of pretentious souls.
Yes, I am an introvert
and I am not ashamed of it.
I'm rather proud that
I am more than enough for me.

296.

Find someone who
isn't afraid to fall
to make your wish come true,
just like a shooting star.

Love needs courage

297.

The past can haunt you
for as long as you want it to.
The past can stop being a bother
right when you decide to
accept the lesson it taught
and let it go for a better present.

Let past remain in past

298.

Whether you have
a hundred shoulders to lean on
or you have none,
at the end of the day,
you've got to wipe your tears yourself,
you've got to be your own saviour.

Stay strong

299.

If the wrong ones
didn't reject you,
you would have
never found
the right one
and your life
wouldn't have been
this good.

Rejections aren't bad

300.

You're beautiful,
you know?
Maybe their eyes
aren't beautiful enough to behold.

The defect is in their eyes

301.

Your clothes create illusion,
did you know that?
They can make you look
taller or
shorter or
thinner or
fatter.
It's just an illusion.
Focus on your health,
appearance shall manage itself.

Illusion

302.

Pick up your
workout gear,
pull on those
sports clothes
and hit the gym
or the park,
or workout from
the comfort of your home.
But move that body
and stay healthy
because nothing else
matters more.

It's all that matters

303.

If they hit you in the face,
stabbing their back
won't make up for a revenge.
Either forgive and forget
or
fight as fairly as they did.
Either way you come out stronger.

Back-stabbing is cowardice

304.

Letting go allows destiny to happen

A dew drop
fell on a leaf,
it rolled down
and hung on the leaf's end.
The leaf kept holding on to it,
trying not to let it drop
and caress the earth,
but the drop fell anyway.
Likewise, in life,
we need to stop
holding on to the people
who are meant to be
with someone else.
When they are on
the edge of leaving,
just set them free
and make space for

who you're meant to be with

for the eternity.

305.

Going through that phase
required a lot of pain
but then,
you gathered your strength
and made your way
through it each day.
The pain
never went in vain;
it made you stronger
and a damn lot wiser.

Stronger

306.

Perfection is a process, not destination

What is perfection?
How can something or someone
achieve perfection
when there is always…
always plenty of room for improvement.
I think perfection is when
you improve yourself a little each day
and become your better self
than the previous one.
Perfection cannot be achieved;
perfection, for me, is a process,
the process of grinding each day
and bringing out the best in you.

307.

Listen,

go hydrate yourself.

The world that broke you

won't look after you.

You've got to be there

for yourself and your needs,

only you can make you

healthy and strong.

Come back stronger each time

the world tries to dim your shine.

Make yourself whole again

308.

It’s the memories
that keep a person
alive in someone’s heart.

309.

You doubting yourself is
an advantage for others.

Imposter syndrome

310.

There will always be haters

There will always be haters,
it's a harsh truth, I know
but accepting their existence
and ignoring it all the same
increases your productivity
instead of worrying about them.

Our mind somehow
gives more importance
to the negative ones
but also,
we can reprogram it
to accept and forget haters
and focus only on the positives.

How can you let down
a million lovers of your art

just because

a few mean clowns

want your success to drown?

311.

It's O.K. to have scars,
we all have them.
But it's not okay
to intentionally be
the reason behind
someone else's scars.

Know the difference

312.

Life breaks to make

Life breaks.
It breaks everyone,
but it breaks the most
the ones who are the strongest of all.
Yes, the strongest ones
have been through the worst.
Because it's life,
and life has this habit;
the habit of breaking us
before making us.

313.

Your mental health
is more important than
everything else in your life,
including the people
you're trying so hard to please.

314.

Lessons learned from nature

When the chaos of the city life
becomes too overwhelming,
switch to the nature,
stand face-to-face with it,
and see,
it gives so many lessons for free.
The Moon teaches us
to go gracefully through the phases.
The Sun teaches us
to shine even when we're burning.
The mountains show us
how to stand tall
no matter how tough it gets.
The ocean takes every shape
teaching us to be flexible
despite being so vast and reverential.
The flowers show us how to
beautifully add scent to the lives of others
even if our own is filled with thorns,
even if we're being dried,
destroyed, and plucked.

The earth and the sky
show us the power
of being in love from a distance,
embracing separation
so that the world can survive
with perfect synchronisation.

315.

Making fun of someone
and belittling them
won't make you look cool,
but having fun with them
and your ability to
laugh at yourself
will sure do.

Don't make anyone's fun

316.

And when someone's gone,
you miss even the fights that
you used to have with them.

317.

Once the damage has been done,
you may try your best to keep it hidden
but you can never hide from the One
watching over all of us.

318.

If you have the two choices: you may work at a job you love but pays a little or you may work at a job you hate but pays luxuriously, which one would you choose?

If you chose the first, are able to pay your bills and lead a happy life, keep going. It's the best. Now coming to the next. Isn't it ironic? You work at a job you hate to get a luxurious life? Grinding at a place you're not happy at is the first step towards snatching the luxury of happiness and satisfaction from yourself. Even if you want that luxury for your family, I'm sure your family would love to see you happy first, miserable for luxury later.

319.

When they do you bad,
God stands on your side
and holds your hand.

320.

There are three types of people:

Who tell you you're beautiful and compliment you.

Who remain quiet and silently adore the miracle that you are. Maybe they're shy to express, maybe they do not want you to know that they are inspired by you.

Who throw hatred and jealousy in their comments while in their heart, they do know how amazing you are.

People aren't always (dis)honest

321.

A change in year
can't change you
only you can change you
because the change
begins with you.

322.

Too many untold stories lie
buried under the forgotten ruins.

323.

Time and experience
change your perception
towards almost
everything in life.

324.

Let's loosen a bit

The world expects
a lot from us
and it's not our job
to fulfil their unreal hopes.
But there's something
that we need to think.
Sometimes,
our own expectations
from ourselves
become unreal too.
We wish to achieve a lot,
only pushing ourselves
on the edge of
the risk of falling
because believe me,
chasing one achievable goal
is far more satisfying

than crying over

a bunch of unrealistic

expectations, dreams and hopes.

325.

Goodbyes

Whether it's losing
your beloved to someone else
or losing your loved ones
to the Almighty,
goodbyes are hard.
Tears keep coming
uninvited in your eyes.
You don't want to
welcome them
but you have to.
Tears are a reminder that
you are capable of
tolerating the pain.
Yes, people might think
you are sensitive,
but how does that matter?
It's OK to mourn the loss.

After all,

some goodbyes are permanent.

326.

As long as you keep
needing permission for everything,
you'll remain a slave to others.

327.

Understanding is tough at times

but being understood is tougher.

328.

Pond or ocean?

We all have
a pond-like mind;
a single provocation
from someone or something
disturbs our mental peace
like a small pebble
creates ripples in a pond.

Ocean has a lot to teach;
even when a whole river
flows into it,
it remains calm,
such is its majesty
and such is the power
of an oceanic mind.
No negativity,
no anger, no hatred

can ever disturb its peace.

So, which is yours—
a pond-like mind
or an oceanic one?
Mine sure is pond-like
but maybe someday
when I have reached
the highest level of
accepting things,
situations and people
the way they are,
I'll also find
all the peace
of my mind.

329.

Runner and chaser

You chase them
as much as you want to
but it is also true
that they will return to you
the day when you
give up on the chase
and start being
busy with your life.
I bet you'll see
how the runner and the chaser
switch the damn positions;
how, now, they'll chase you
and you will want to run away.
Life is funny,
it works in weird ways.

330.

Faces are never
beautiful or ugly,
minds are.

331.

True, writers write for themselves
but it's also true that their words
reach the destination only when
their readers find their words relatable.

Thank you, readers

With acceptance,

life becomes

a thousandfold easier.

Healing

ABOUT THE AUTHOR

Shilpa Goel is the author of Poetic Letters To God, The Book of Infinite Writing Prompts and Trusting God: The Path of Least Resistance. From being clueless about life to finding a purpose, poetry and writing have been her greatest assets. Shilpa has compiled and edited five anthologies of poems and short stories about romance and travels. Her work has been published in eight anthologies. Shilpa shares her poetry, prose, and quotes regularly on Instagram and has readers from all over the world.

She has been listed among top 10 on the list of 31 Modern Poets You Should Follow by glowhabits.com and has been featured in Media Talk Back magazine by MESC India.

Besides writing, she loves journaling, reading, blogging, content writing, travelling, and being surrounded by nature.

More Books by Shilpa Goel

- *Poetic Letters To God*
- *The Book of Infinite Writing Prompts*
- *Trusting God:The Path Of Least Resistance*

Available worldwide on Amazon.

Meetlife Journals

available on

amazon.com

&

notionpress.com

Instagram: @journalsplanners

9 789334 421460